rib-ticklers M+A-T-H

Strengthening Basic Skills with Jokes, Comics, and Riddles

GRADE 2

Credits

Author: Darcy Andries

Editor: JulieAnna Kirsch

Cover and Layout Design: Chasity Rice

Inside Illustrations: Robbie Short

Cover Illustration: Rich Powell

This book has been correlated to state, national, and Canadian provincial standards. Visit *www.carsondellosa.com* to search for and view its correlations to your standards.

Printed in the USA • All rights reserved.   ISBN: 978-1-60418-139-5

Table of Contents

Skills Matrix (Based on NCTM Content Strands)

Page Number	Number & Operations	Algebra	Geometry	Measurement	Data Analysis & Probability
4	√				
5	√				
6	√				
7	√				
8	√				
9	√				
10	√				
11	√				
12	√				
13	√				
14	√				
15	√				
16	√				
17	√				
18	√				
19	√				
20	√				
21	√				
22	√				
23	√				
24	√				
25	√				
26	√				
27	√				
28	√				
29	√				
30	√				
31	√				
32	√				
33				√	
34				√	
35				√	
36				√	
37				√	
38				√	

Page Number	Number & Operations	Algebra	Geometry	Measurement	Data Analysis & Probability
39				√	
40				√	
41				√	
42				√	
43				√	
44	√				
45	√				
46	√				
47	√				
48	√				
49	√				
50	√				
51	√				
52	√				
53	√				
54	√				
55	√				
56		√			
57		√			
58		√			
59		√			
60		√			
61		√			
62		√			
63		√			
64			√		
65			√		
66			√		
67			√		
68			√		
69					√
70					√
71					√
72					√
73					√

Word for Word

Write the numbers as words. Find each word in the word search.

1. 13 _____ 2. 42 _____

3. 87 _____ 4. 106 _____

5. 200 _____ 6. 310 _____

7. 400 _____ 8. 500 _____

9. 800 _____ 10. 1,000 _____

```
e  i  g  h  t  h  u  n  d  r  e  d  h  r  o
r  y  m  v  w  u  j  e  p  l  q  a  i  t  n
l  v  b  u  o  k  t  m  y  a  d  o  q  i  e
f  i  v  e  h  u  n  d  r  e  d  l  k  e  t
x  s  b  m  u  l  a  w  n  j  y  a  p  i  h
c  n  p  t  n  x  r  k  s  t  e  f  x  g  o
e  g  d  e  d  j  n  g  u  d  u  h  z  h  u
f  f  o  u  r  h  u  n  d  r  e  d  v  t  s
o  e  r  x  e  m  a  o  h  b  a  u  n  y  a
r  b  a  p  d  z  d  y  k  g  w  k  p  s  n
t  h  i  r  t  e  e  n  t  d  f  o  v  e  d
y  d  l  g  r  p  y  h  e  b  m  y  a  v  j
t  h  r  e  e  h  u  n  d  r  e  d  t  e  n
w  s  v  z  k  t  n  m  q  g  r  p  d  n  a
o  n  e  h  u  n  d  r  e  d  s  i  x  e  l
```

4

You "Quack" Me Up

Write each group of four numbers in order from least to greatest. To solve the riddles, write each letter beneath its number.

1. What do you need when your sneakers fall apart?

   103 **O**   33 **S**   220 **E**   92 **H**   153 **U**   172 **E**   127 **L**   99 **G**

   ___ ___ ___ ___   ___ ___ ___ ___

   ___ ___ ___ ___   ___ ___ ___ ___

2. What do you call a faded bucket?

   234 **A**   285 **E**   250 **L**   201 **P**   346 **L**   311 **A**   296 **P**   339 **I**

   ___ ___ ___ ___   ___ ___ ___ ___

   ___ ___ ___ ___   ___ ___ ___ ___

3. What do you call a baby deer in your front yard?

   367 **A**   376 **W**   377 **N**   364 **L**   425 **A**   414 **F**   499 **N**   440 **W**

   ___ ___ ___ ___   ___ ___ ___ ___

   ___ ___ ___ ___   ___ ___ ___ ___

Odds and Evens

Color the spaces with odd numbers blue. Color the spaces with even numbers orange. The picture will solve the riddle.

I never ask questions, but I always get answered. What am I?

13
1
21
2
36
91
33
10
44
22
142
58
76
104
87
60
124
130
92
45
80
112
79
57
69

All Mixed Up

Unscramble the words to spell the ordinal number that comes after each number in parentheses.

1. (75th) vstyeen-xsiht _____

2. (44th) trfoy-fihft _____

3. (36th) ttrihy-hevtsen _____

4. (58th) yftif-hinnt _____

5. (97th) tnenyi-gheiht _____

6. (63rd) xysti-rhtuof _____

7. (79th) eeghhiitt _____

8. (12th) eehhinrttt _____

9. (29th) ehhiirttt _____

10. (51st) fiytf-ecsdno _____

Shake, Rattle, and Roll

Use >, <, or = to compare each pair of numbers. Color spaces with > orange. Color spaces with < green. Color spaces with = blue. The picture will solve the riddle.

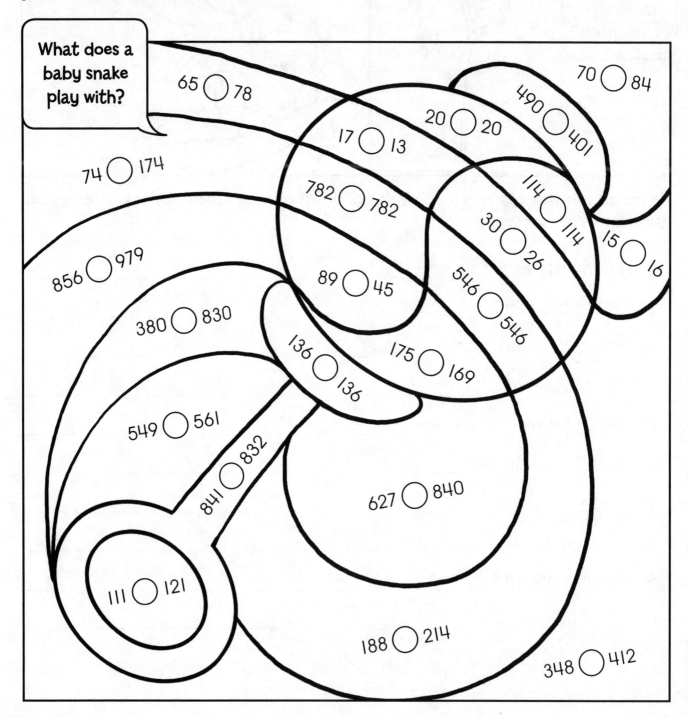

What does a baby snake play with?

65 ◯ 78

70 ◯ 84

490 ◯ 401

20 ◯ 20

17 ◯ 13

114 ◯ 114

74 ◯ 174

782 ◯ 782

30 ◯ 26

15 ◯ 16

856 ◯ 979

89 ◯ 45

546 ◯ 546

380 ◯ 830

136 ◯ 136

175 ◯ 169

549 ◯ 561

841 ◯ 832

627 ◯ 840

111 ◯ 121

188 ◯ 214

348 ◯ 412

Numbers Rock!

Find the place value of each underlined number. Circle the answer. To solve the riddle, write the letter of each circled answer in order on the answer lines.

1. 4,3_8_9
    N. ones
    R. tens
    E. thousands

2. 1,_7_08
    G. ones
    P. tens
    O. hundreds

3. 97_1_
    C. ones
    E. tens
    S. hundreds

4. 6,2_4_2
    B. ones
    K. tens
    W. thousands

5. _7_,906
    A. tens
    F. hundreds
    G. thousands

6. 5,36_4_
    R. ones
    S. tens
    V. hundreds

7. 8,_7_50
    M. tens
    O. hundreds
    Z. thousands

8. 9,8_1_0
    U. tens
    T. hundreds
    Y. thousands

9. _7_,803
    I. tens
    N. hundreds
    P. thousands

What do you call three stones with electric guitars?

Answer: A " ___ ___ ___ ___ " ___ ___ ___ ___ ___

Hungry for Numbers

Write the missing numbers.

Before	Between	After
1. _____ 10	2. 10 _____ 12	3. 12 _____
4. _____ 5	5. 5 _____ 7	6. 7 _____
7. _____ 39	8. 39 _____ 41	9. 41 _____
10. _____ 14	11. 14 _____ 16	12. 16 _____
13. _____ 20	14. 20 _____ 22	15. 22 _____

To solve the riddle, write the number between 7 and 9.

Answer: Because 7 "_____" 9.

Thomas Tomato

Add to find each sum. To solve the riddle, match the sums to the numbers below. Then, write the correct letter on each answer line. Hint: Not all of the letters will be used. Some of the letters will be used more than once.

1. $\begin{array}{r} 13 \\ + 1 \\ \hline \end{array}$ **A**

2. $\begin{array}{r} 16 \\ + 2 \\ \hline \end{array}$ **D**

3. $\begin{array}{r} 8 \\ + 5 \\ \hline \end{array}$ **E**

4. $\begin{array}{r} 11 \\ + 5 \\ \hline \end{array}$ **H**

5. $\begin{array}{r} 5 \\ + 5 \\ \hline \end{array}$ **I**

6. $\begin{array}{r} 11 \\ + 6 \\ \hline \end{array}$ **K**

7. $\begin{array}{r} 6 \\ + 9 \\ \hline \end{array}$ **L**

8. $\begin{array}{r} 5 \\ + 4 \\ \hline \end{array}$ **M**

9. $\begin{array}{r} 13 \\ + 7 \\ \hline \end{array}$ **N**

10. $\begin{array}{r} 7 \\ + 1 \\ \hline \end{array}$ **O**

11. $\begin{array}{r} 3 \\ + 3 \\ \hline \end{array}$ **P**

12. $\begin{array}{r} 1 \\ + 1 \\ \hline \end{array}$ **R**

13. $\begin{array}{r} 10 \\ + 1 \\ \hline \end{array}$ **S**

14. $\begin{array}{r} 12 \\ + 7 \\ \hline \end{array}$ **T**

15. $\begin{array}{r} 2 \\ + 2 \\ \hline \end{array}$ **W**

How do you fix a tomato with a broken foot?

Answer: ___ ___ ___ ___
       4   10   19   16

___ ___ ___ ___ ___ ___   ___ ___ ___ ___ ___
19   8   9   14   19   8   6   14   11   19   13

Way to "Bee"

Add to find each sum. To solve the riddle, match each sum with the correct letter in the key. Then, write the letters in order on the answer lines.

27 = B	55 = H	56 = N	68 = C	79 = E
81 = Y	82 = O	86 = S	90 = A	94 = M

1. 35
    + 20

2. 53
    + 26

3. 34
    + 21

4. 50
    + 40

5. 63
    + 23

6. 60
    + 30

7. 34
    + 21

8. 71
    + 11

9. 21
    + 35

10. 52
    + 27

11. 60
    + 21

12. 24
    + 44

13. 50
    + 32

14. 71
    + 23

15. 15
    + 12

Why does the bee have sticky hair?

Answer: ____ ____ ____ ____ ____

____ "____ ____ ____ ____ ____ - ____ ____ ____ ____."

Name: _____

Music to My Ears

Add to find each sum. To solve the riddle, match the sums to the numbers below. Then, write the correct letter on each answer line. Hint: Some letters will be used more than once.

1. 200
   + 333
   A

2. 104
   + 131
   B

3. 102
   + 90
   D

4. 272
   + 210
   E

5. 501
   + 77
   H

6. 231
   + 60
   I

7. 352
   + 406
   L

8. 723
   + 255
   N

9. 327
   + 170
   O

10. 510
   + 233
   P

11. 573
   + 321
   T

12. 122
   + 203
   W

13. 201
   + 416
   Y

14. 534
   + 335
   R

Why did the man lay his head on the piano?

Answer: ____ ____   ____ ____ ____ ____ ____ ____   ____ ____
          578   482   325   533   978   894   482   192   894   497

" ____ ____ ____ ____   ____ ____   ____ ____   ____ ____ ____ . "
  743   758   533   617   291   894   235   617   482   533   869

Name: _____

On the Go

Add to find each sum.

1. Aiden rides the bus 112 blocks to school. Kaylee rides the bus 67 blocks to school. How many total blocks do Aiden and Kaylee ride the bus to school?

2. Devon's class is visiting the zoo. At the zoo, Devon counts 123 birds and 55 monkeys. How many birds and monkeys does Devon count in all?

3. Ava's class is visiting a museum. At the museum, Ava counts 103 paintings and 206 sculptures. How many total paintings and sculptures does Ava count?

4. Olivia's school has two buses. Each bus takes 40 students to school every morning. Altogether, how many students do the buses take to school each day?

Jayla's Journey

Help Jayla get to the playground. Draw a line through the problems with correct sums.

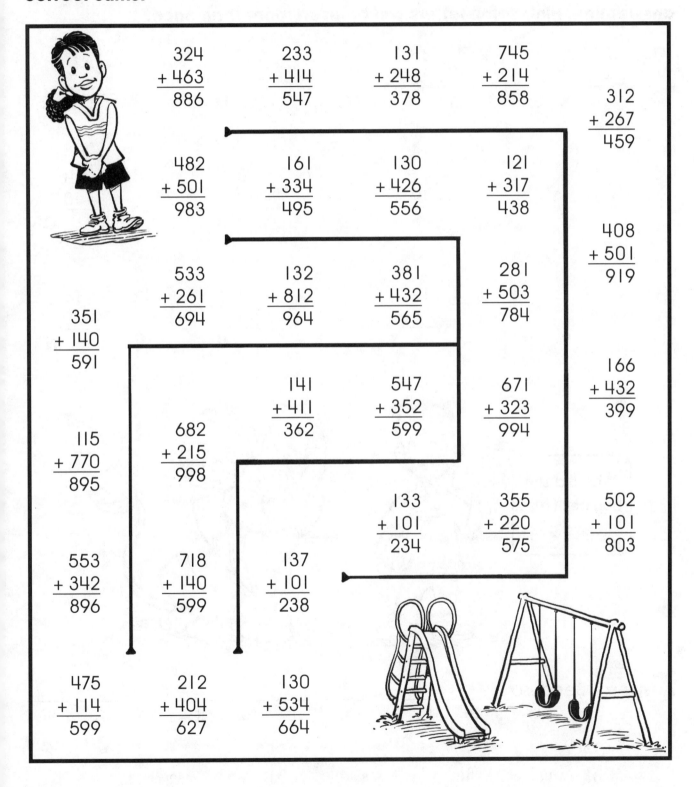

324 + 463 886	233 + 414 547	131 + 248 378	745 + 214 858	
				312 + 267 459
482 + 501 983	161 + 334 495	130 + 426 556	121 + 317 438	
				408 + 501 919

351
+ 140
591

533   132   381   281
+ 261   + 812   + 432   + 503
694   964   565   784

166
+ 432
399

115
+ 770
895

682
+ 215
998

141   547   671
+ 411   + 352   + 323
362   599   994

133   355   502
+ 101   + 220   + 101
234   575   803

553   718   137
+ 342   + 140   + 101
896   599   238

475   212   130
+ 114   + 404   + 534
599   627   664

Tall Tales

Add to find each sum. Regroup if necessary. To solve the riddle, match the sums to the numbers below. Then, write the correct letter on each answer line. Hint: Some letters will be used more than once.

1.	2.	3.	4.
19 + 2 **A**	36 + 6 **E**	32 + 8 **G**	17 + 3 **H**

5.	6.	7.	8.
16 + 17 **I**	12 + 19 **L**	18 + 12 **N**	14 + 18 **O**

9.	10.	11.	12.
39 + 49 **S**	19 + 26 **T**	17 + 26 **U**	18 + 23 **W**

Why did the boy not trust the pig?

Answer: Because ___ ___   ___ ___ ___ ___ ___ ___ ___
                    20 42   45 20 32 43 40 20 45

 ___ ___   ___ ___ ___ ___ ___ ___ ___
 33 45   41 21 88   31 33 32 30

Elephant Antics

Add to find each sum. Regroup if necessary. To solve the riddle, match the sums to the numbers below. Then, write the correct letter on each answer line. Hint: Some letters will be used more than once.

1.	48	2.	52	3.	42	4.	47
	+ 14		+ 34		+ 38		+ 18
	A		**C**		**E**		**G**

5.	11	6.	39	7.	28	8.	13
	+ 29		+ 16		+ 16		+ 29
	I		**M**		**N**		**O**

9.	26	10.	25	11.	41
	+ 47		+ 66		+ 19
	T		**R**		**W**

What time is it when there is an elephant in your car?

Answer: ___ ___ ___ ___   ___ ___   ___ ___ ___
73 40 55 80   73 42   65 80 73

___   ___ ___ ___   ___ ___ ___
62   44 80 60   86 62 91

An Apple a Day

What type of fruit tree lines up in groups of two?

"Pair" trees!

Add to find each sum. Regroup if necessary.

1. Mrs. Jones uses 34 red apples and 8 green apples to make juice. How many apples does she use in all?

2. Gabriel sells pears at the farmers' market. On Saturday, he sold 41 pears. On Sunday, he sold 29 pears. How many pears did he sell in all?

3. Anna baked 14 apple pies on Tuesday and 17 peach pies on Wednesday. How many pies did Anna bake in all?

4. Julian has 32 apple trees and 49 pear trees. How many trees does he have in all?

Name: _____   addition

Along for the Ride

Add to find each sum. Regroup if necessary. To solve the riddle, match the sums to the numbers below. Then, write the correct letter on each answer line. Hint: Not all of the letters will be used. Some of the letters will be used more than once.

1. 19
   + 81
    A

2. 158
   + 27
    B

3. 256
   + 35
    C

4. 151
   + 98
    D

5. 566
   + 35
    E

6. 470
   + 56
    H

7. 275
   + 43
    I

8. 197
   + 191
    L

9. 163
   + 62
    N

10. 525
   + 173
    O

11. 173
   + 445
    R

12. 286
   + 53
    S

13. 255
   + 573
    T

14. 207
   + 523
    V

15. 335
   + 629
    W

Why did the man put his car in the refrigerator?

Answer: Because ___ ___   ___ ___ ___ ___ ___ ___
            526 601   964 100 225 828 601 249

___ " ___ ___ ___ " ___ ___ ___ ___
100   291 698 698 388   618 318 249 601

Rib-Ticklers Math   **19**   © Carson-Dellosa • CD-104285

By the Numbers

Add to find each sum. Use the sums to complete the crossword puzzle.

Across

2. 514
    + 437

3. 321
    + 491

4. 147
    + 318

7. 592
    + 321

9. 649
    + 122

11. 464
     + 185

12. 132
     + 149

13. 138
     + 170

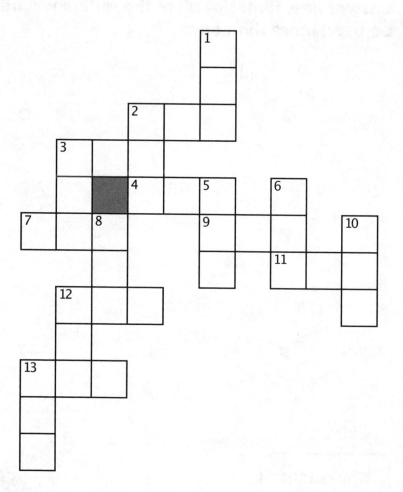

Down

1. 256
    + 35

2. 692
    + 232

3. 445
    + 416

5. 338
    + 235

6. 240
    + 176

8. 275
    + 63

10. 316
     + 274

12. 142
     + 138

13. 211
     + 129

Tasty Treats

What do you call a train loaded with bubble gum?

A "chew-chew" train!

Add to find each sum. Regroup if necessary.

1. Tyrone has 37 cherries and 44 grapes. How many cherries and grapes does Tyrone have in all?

2. Lisa is bringing snacks for her class. She has 72 granola bars and 59 apples. How many granola bars and apples does Lisa have in all?

3. Amy has two bags of carrot sticks. The first bag has 141 carrot sticks. The second bag has 129 carrot sticks. How many total carrot sticks does Amy have?

4. Marcus has two bags of jelly beans. The first bag has 188 jelly beans. The second bag has 80 jelly beans. How many jelly beans does Marcus have in all?

Clever Kangaroos

Subtract to find each difference. To solve the riddle, match the differences to the numbers below. Then, write the correct letter on each answer line. Hint: Some of the letters will be used more than once.

1. 19 − 1 **S**	2. 11 − 1 **O**	3. 9 − 3 **I**	4. 19 −10 **D**
5. 18 − 2 **A**	6. 13 − 2 **C**	7. 18 − 3 **T**	8. 17 − 3 **R**
9. 17 −10 **P**	10. 13 − 1 **N**	11. 19 −11 **K**	12. 18 − 5 **E**

Where do kangaroos find the meanings of words?

Answer: ___ ___ " ___ ___ ___ ___ ___ ___ "
      6   12   7   10   11   8   13   15

___ ___ ___ ___ ___ ___ ___ ___ ___ ___ ___ ___
 9   6   11   15   6   10   12   16   14   6   13   18

They Are All Ears

Subtract to find each difference.

1. Martin has 55 bean stalks. Twelve of them fall over during a storm. How many bean stalks does Martin have left?

2. Natalie plants 54 sunflower seeds. Only 44 of the seeds sprout. How many sunflower seeds do not sprout?

3. Jonathan has 17 tomato plants in his garden. He gives 5 tomato plants to his friend Roy. How many tomato plants does Jonathan have left?

4. Ella picks 87 strawberries on Thursday and 76 strawberries on Friday. How many more strawberries did Ella pick on Thursday than on Friday?

Name: _____

Flying High

Subtract to find each difference. To solve the riddle, match each difference with the correct letter in the key. Then, write the letters in order on the answer lines.

12 = F	14 = Y	23 = G	25 = I	29 = N	31 = R
33 = C	44 = A	50 = T	56 = L	61 = P	72 = E

1. 77
   − 33

2. 39
   − 27

3. 99
   − 43

4. 25
   − 11

5. 96
   − 71

6. 79
   − 50

7. 79
   − 56

8. 76
   − 43

9. 97
   − 53

10. 51
   − 20

11. 85
   − 24

12. 87
   − 15

13. 86
   − 36

What do you get when you cross a dog, a bird, and a car?

Answer: ____ _____ _____ _____ _____

"____ ____ - ____ ____ ____"

Rib-Ticklers Math

© Carson-Dellosa • CD-104285

Show Business

Subtract to find each difference. To solve the riddle, match each difference with the correct letter in the key. Then, write the letters in order on the answer lines.

51 = U	105 = D	121 = E	142 = M	313 = S	330 = H
334 = F	404 = N	514 = I	529 = C	542 = O	610 = T

1. 630
    − 20

2. 990
    − 660

3. 527
    − 406

4. 799
    − 469

5. 888
    − 346

6. 194
    − 143

7. 617
    − 213

8. 867
    − 762

9. 593
    − 51

10. 575
    − 241

11. 442
    − 300

12. 775
    − 724

13. 778
    − 465

14. 635
    − 121

15. 659
    − 130

What is a dog's favorite musical?

Answer: ___ ___ ___   " ___ ___ ___ ___ ___ "

___ ___ ___   ___ ___ ___ ___ ___

Movie Magic

Subtract to find each difference.

1. David wants to see a movie that is playing at two different theaters. The Regency Theater is 49 miles away. The Grand Theater is 35 miles away. How much farther away is the Regency Theater than the Grand Theater?

2. On Sunday, 744 people saw "Sleepless in the Saddle." Fourteen people fell asleep during the movie. How many people did not fall asleep during the movie?

3. On Saturday, 971 people went to see "Bee Your Best." On Sunday, 320 people saw the same movie. How many more people saw the movie on Saturday than on Sunday?

4. On Friday, 974 people saw "The Umpire Strikes Back." On Saturday, 813 people saw the same movie. How many more people saw the movie on Friday than on Saturday?

Sweet Dreams

Subtract to find each difference. Regroup if necessary. To solve the riddle, match each difference with the correct letter in the key. Then, write the letters in order on the answer lines.

12 = C	13 = K	16 = I	18 = O
19 = E	26 = T	28 = H	29 = S

1. 21
  − 9

2. 25
  − 7

3. 27
  − 9

4. 21
  − 8

5. 23
  − 7

6. 25
  − 6

7. 32
  − 3

8. 32
  − 4

9. 21
  − 2

10. 24
  − 5

11. 33
  − 7

12. 34
  − 5

What do gingerbread men keep on their beds?

Answer: ____ ____ ____ ____ ____

" ____ ____ ____ ____ ____ ____ "

The Moo's News

Subtract to find each difference. Regroup if necessary. To solve the riddle, match each difference with the correct letter in the key. Then, write the letters in order on the answer lines.

8 = E	9 = P	11 = I	13 = R	14 = M
18 = S	19 = O	24 = A	29 = N	

1. 50
   − 39

2. 46
   − 17

3. 50
   − 26

4. 32
   − 18

5. 66
   − 47

6. 45
   − 26

7. 34
   − 16

8. 77
   − 68

9. 63
   − 39

10. 36
   − 27

11. 52
   − 44

12. 41
   − 28

Where can you read about famous cows?

Answer: ____ ____   ____

" ____ ____ ____ ____ – ____ ____ ____ ____ ____ "

28

In Full Bloom

Subtract to find each difference. Regroup if necessary.

1. Eli counts 22 hummingbirds in his flower bed. Thirteen of the hummingbirds are blue. How many of the hummingbirds are not blue?

2. Nancy has two rosebushes. One rosebush has 31 red roses on it. The other rosebush has 19 white roses on it. How many more red roses than white roses does Nancy have?

3. Brooke plants 35 flowers in her garden and 29 flowers around her mailbox. How many more flowers are in her garden than around her mailbox?

4. Jake counts 28 ladybugs in his vegetable garden and 19 ladybugs in his flower bed. How many more ladybugs are in the vegetable garden than in the flower bed?

On the "Moove"

Subtract to find each difference. Regroup if necessary. To solve the riddle, match the differences to the numbers below. Then, write the correct letter on each answer line. Hint: Not all of the letters will be used. Some of the letters will be used more than once.

1. $\begin{array}{r} 151 \\ -\ 68 \\ \hline \end{array}$ **A**	2. $\begin{array}{r} 382 \\ -\ 69 \\ \hline \end{array}$ **B**	3. $\begin{array}{r} 728 \\ -\ 19 \\ \hline \end{array}$ **C**	4. $\begin{array}{r} 581 \\ -\ 49 \\ \hline \end{array}$ **E**
5. $\begin{array}{r} 265 \\ -\ 19 \\ \hline \end{array}$ **I**	6. $\begin{array}{r} 841 \\ -\ 23 \\ \hline \end{array}$ **L**	7. $\begin{array}{r} 241 \\ -127 \\ \hline \end{array}$ **M**	8. $\begin{array}{r} 580 \\ -354 \\ \hline \end{array}$ **N**
9. $\begin{array}{r} 768 \\ -329 \\ \hline \end{array}$ **O**	10. $\begin{array}{r} 631 \\ -526 \\ \hline \end{array}$ **T**	11. $\begin{array}{r} 495 \\ -347 \\ \hline \end{array}$ **W**	12. $\begin{array}{r} 989 \\ -898 \\ \hline \end{array}$ **Y**

What has two wheels and gives milk?

Answer:

___	___	___	___		___	___		___
83	709	439	148		439	226		83

___	___	___	___	___	___	___
313	246	709	91	709	818	532

Bound Around

Subtract to find each difference. If you regroup to solve the problem, color the space brown. If you do not regroup, color the space blue. The picture will solve the riddle.

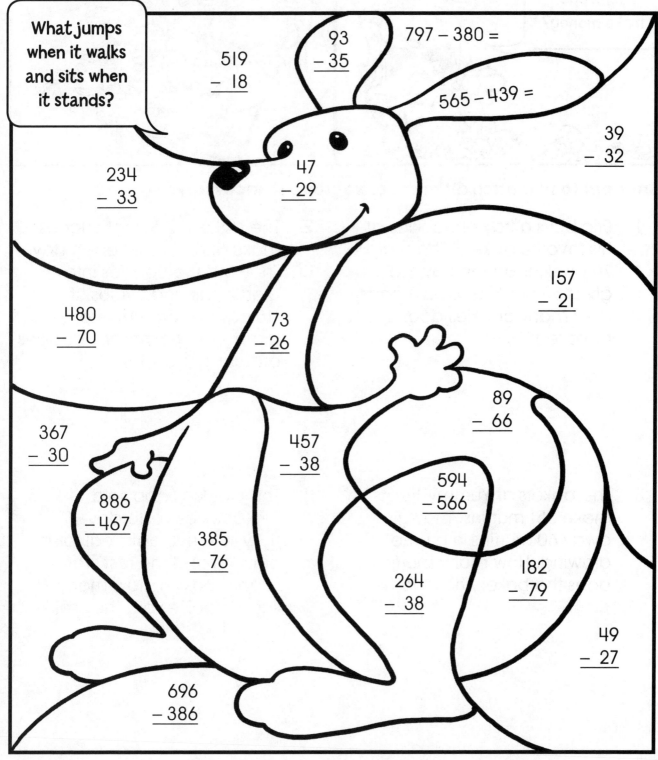

What jumps when it walks and sits when it stands?

797 − 380 =

565 − 439 =

93
− 35

519
− 18

47
− 29

39
− 32

234
− 33

157
− 21

480
− 70

73
− 26

89
− 66

367
− 30

457
− 38

594
− 566

886
− 467

182
− 79

385
− 76

264
− 38

49
− 27

696
− 386

Sweet Success

Subtract to find each difference. Regroup if necessary.

1. Eric buys a tray of cookies at his favorite bakery. There are 74 cookies on the tray. He gives 55 cookies to his friends. How many cookies does Eric have left?

2. The bakers at Sweet Success make 320 cookies each day. They cut the cookies into diamonds and circles. If 115 cookies are cut into diamonds, how many cookies are cut into circles?

3. The bakers at Yummy Treats make 351 muffins. They give away 60 muffins in a prize drawing. How many muffins does the bakery have left?

4. The Cookie Shop sold 996 cookies yesterday. If they sold 498 oatmeal raisin cookies and the rest were sugar cookies, how many sugar cookies did they sell?

Farmer Leslie's Fences

What runs around a field but never moves?

A fence!

Help Farmer Leslie build new fences around her pastures. Find the perimeter of each shape.

1.
3 yd.

2 yd.

P = _____ yd.

2.
6 ft.

2 ft.

P = _____ ft.

3.
5 ft.

4 ft.

P = _____ ft.

4.
10 yd.

10 yd.

P = _____ yd.

5.
7 ft.

5 ft.

P = _____ ft.

6.
5 ft.

5 ft.

P = _____ ft.

7.
5 yd.

3 yd.

P = _____ yd.

8.
10 ft.

4 ft.

P = _____ ft.

Under the Weather

Help Carlos decide what to wear. Write the temperatures shown on each thermometer on the answer lines. Then, circle the clothing that Carlos should wear that day.

1.
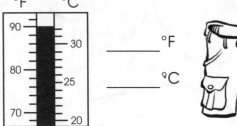

_____ °F

_____ °C

2.
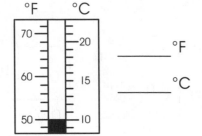

_____ °F

_____ °C

3.
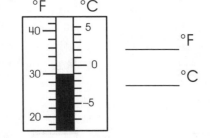

_____ °F

_____ °C

4.
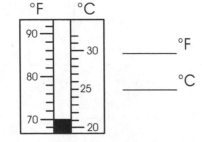

_____ °F

_____ °C

For the Record

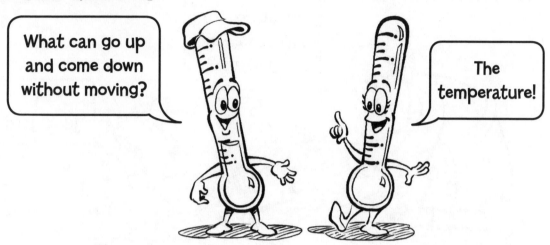

Color each thermometer to match the temperature given.

1. 0°C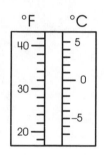

2. 86°F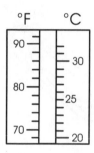

3. 25°C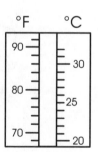

4. 58°F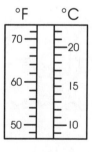

5. 29°C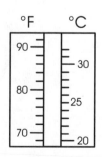

6. 60°F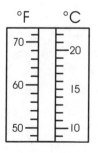

Name: _____

 measurement

The Whole Nine Yards

Circle the best unit of measurement for each object.

1.

in.　　ft.　　yd.

2.

in.　　ft.　　yd.

3.

in.　　ft.　　yd.

4.

in.　　ft.　　yd.

5.

in.　　ft.　　yd.

6.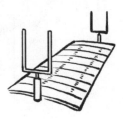

in.　　ft.　　yd.

7.

in.　　ft.　　yd.

8.

in.　　ft.　　yd.

9.

in.　　ft.　　yd.

Rib-Ticklers Math　　　　**36**　　　© Carson-Dellosa • CD-104285

The Long and Short of It

Circle the best unit of measurement for each object.

1.

cm   m

2.

cm   m

3.

cm   m

4.

cm   m

5.

cm   m

6.

cm   m

7.

cm   m

8.

cm   m

9.

cm   m

Allie's Busy Day

Help Allie find her way home. Draw a line through the clocks that show time getting later by 30 minutes.

Only a Matter of Time

Owen has a busy schedule today. Draw how each clock will look when it is time for the activity.

1. wake up—7:15

2. eat breakfast—7:30

3. get to school—8:15

4. eat lunch—11:45

5. go home—3:15

6. do chores —4:45

7. eat dinner—5:45

8. walk Fido—6:15

9. go to bed—9:30

Name: _____

Have You "Herd"?

Write the time beneath each clock. To solve the riddle, match the answers to the times below. Then, write the correct letter on each answer line.

1.

_____ **A**

2.

_____ **E**

3.

_____ **F**

4.

_____ **N**

5.

_____ **O**

6.

_____ **R**

7.

_____ **T**

What time is it when 10 elephants are following you?

Answer: ___ ___ ___
5:40   2:25   6:55

___ ___ ___ ___ ___   ___ ___ ___
9:50 9:10 5:40 2:25 10:20   2:45 6:55 2:25

Knight Time

Write the time beneath each clock. To solve the riddle, match the answers to the times below. Then, write the correct letter on each answer line.

1.

_____ **A**

2.

_____ **I**

3.

_____ **F**

4.

_____ **S**

5.

_____ **T**

6.

_____ **R**

7.

_____ **U**

8.

_____ **O**

9.

_____ **M**

What did Sir Lancelot wear to dinner?

Answer: ____ " ____ ____ ____ ____ "

4:10   3:05   11:20 10:55 3:25

____ ____   ____ ____ ____ ____ ____

2:15   1:35   4:10   6:50   4:45   2:15   6:50

Like Clockwork

Write the elapsed time in hours and minutes beneath each pair of clocks.
To solve the riddle, match the answers to the times below. Then, write the
correct letter on each answer line. The first one has been done for you.

1.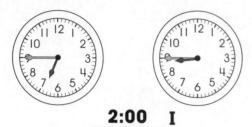

   2:00   **I**

2.

   _____ **D**

3.

   _____ **E**

4.

   _____ **H**

5.

   _____ **A**

6.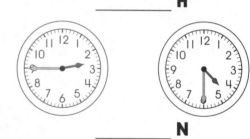

   _____ **N**

7.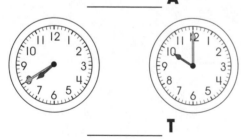

   _____ **T**

Why did the clock stop working?

Answer:

I							
2:00	2:20	1:45	1:15	1:15	2:15	1:15	2:15

	"				"
2:30	0:30	2:30	1:45	2:15	.

Leaps and Bounds

"Leap" years!

What years do frogs love best?

Answer the questions using the calendar below.

February

Sunday	Monday	Tuesday	Wednesday	Thursday	Friday	Saturday
		1	2	3	4	5
6	7	8	9	10	11	12
13	14	15	16	17	18	19
20	21	22	23	24	25	26
27	28					

1. Valentine's Day is February 14. What day of the week is Valentine's Day? _____

2. How many Wednesdays are in February? _____

3. What is the date of the last Saturday in February?

   _____

4. What day of the week will March 1 fall on? _____

5. Imagine that your best friend's birthday is on the second Tuesday of February. What date is her birthday? _____

Rooted in Place

Color the spaces with $\frac{1}{2}$ green. Color the spaces with $\frac{1}{3}$ brown. Color the spaces with $\frac{1}{4}$ blue. The picture will solve the riddle.

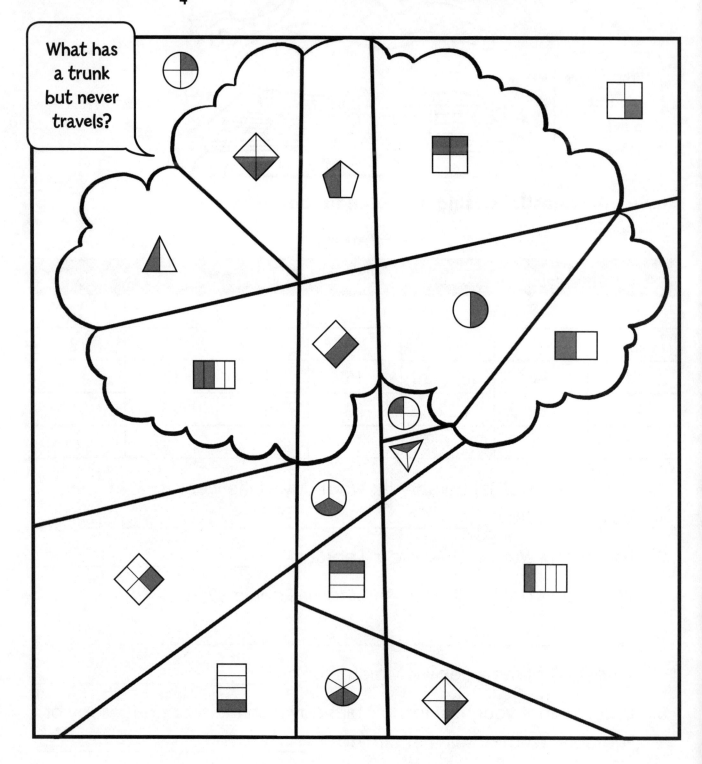

Finding Fractions

Color each circle to illustrate the fraction.

1. $\dfrac{1}{5}$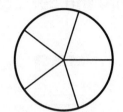

2. $\dfrac{3}{5}$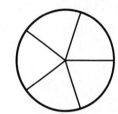

3. $\dfrac{1}{2}$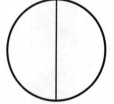

4. $\dfrac{2}{4}$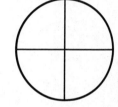

5. $\dfrac{1}{4}$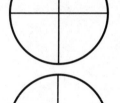

6. $\dfrac{1}{3}$

7. $\dfrac{2}{3}$

8. $\dfrac{2}{5}$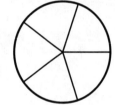

9. $\dfrac{1}{7}$

10. $\dfrac{4}{5}$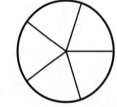

11. $\dfrac{3}{4}$

12. $\dfrac{1}{10}$

13. $\dfrac{1}{6}$

14. $\dfrac{7}{10}$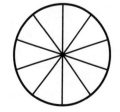

Lumbering Along

Write the fraction shown by each shaded shape. To solve the riddle, match the answers to the fractions below. Then, write the correct letter on each answer line.

1. ___ **I**

2. ___ **W**

3.  ___ **O**

4. ___ **K**

5. ___ **H**

6.  ___ **G**

7. ___ **T**

8. ___ **E**

9.  ___ **N**

10. ___ **O**

11. ___ **R**

How did the tree get lost in the woods?

Answer: ___ ___ ___ ___ ___ ___ ___ ___ ___
$\frac{1}{2}$ $\frac{2}{3}$ $\frac{2}{3}$ $\frac{1}{5}$ $\frac{1}{5}$ $\frac{1}{3}$ $\frac{2}{3}$ $\frac{1}{4}$ $\frac{1}{6}$

___ ___ ___ ___ ___ " ___ ___ ___ ___."
$\frac{3}{4}$ $\frac{5}{6}$ $\frac{1}{5}$ $\frac{4}{5}$ $\frac{3}{5}$ $\frac{5}{6}$ $\frac{1}{5}$ $\frac{1}{5}$ $\frac{2}{3}$

Name: _____   fractions

Easy as Pie

Use >, <, or = to compare each pair of fractions. To solve the riddle, circle the letter next to the fraction that is greater. If the fractions are equivalent, circle both letters. Then, write the circled letters in order on the answer lines.

1. **F** ◯ **Y**   2.  **O** ◯ **U**

3. **N** ◯ **R**   4. **L** ◯ **F**

5. **R** ◯ **O**   6.  **N** ◯ **A**

7. **T** ◯ **N**   8. **S** ◯ **T**

9. **E** ◯ **A**

10. **R** ◯ **E**

11. **T** ◯ **S**

12. **T** ◯ **H**

What is the best thing to put into a pie?

Answer: ___ ___ ___ ___ ___ ___ ___ ___

___ ___ ___ ___ ___

Star Bright

Draw a picture to illustrate each multiplication problem. Then, multiply to find each product.

1. 2 x 2 =   2. 2 x 5 =

3. 3 x 3 =   4. 3 x 2 =

5. 4 x 2 =   6. 2 x 4 =

7. 3 x 4 =   8. 2 x 6 =

Goofy Groceries

Maria is grocery shopping with her mother, Mrs. Diaz. To make the trip more fun, Mrs. Diaz wrote the grocery list in code. Help Maria figure out what items are on the list. Use colorful crayons to connect equivalent problems to their answers. Then, write the three letters in order on the answer lines. The first one has been done for you.

E. 2 + 2 + 2 + 2   I. 2 x 5   M. 4 _____

T. 2 + 2 + 2   G. 2 x 4   M. 2 _____

J. 2 + 2   U. 2 x 1   E. 10 _____

P. 2 + 2 + 2 + 2 + 2   A. 2 x 2   A. 6 _____

G. 2 + 0   E. 2 x 3   G. 8 **EGG**

Leaping Lions

Multiply to find each product. To solve the riddle, match each product with the correct letter in the key. Then, write the letters in order on the answer lines.

8 = H	10 = I	12 = S	15 = W	16 = I	18 = N
20 = S	21 = A	25 = E	27 = N	28 = O	32 = E
35 = L	40 = A	45 = I	50 = T		

1. 5 x 3 = _____

2. 2 x 4 = _____

3. 5 x 5 = _____

4. 3 x 9 = _____

5. 5 x 2 = _____

6. 5 x 10 = _____

7. 2 x 8 = _____

8. 4 x 3 = _____

9. 3 x 7 = _____

10. 4 x 5 = _____

11. 4 x 8 = _____

12. 4 x 10 = _____

13. 5 x 7 = _____

14. 5 x 9 = _____

15. 4 x 7 = _____

16. 3 x 6 = _____

When is a lion not a lion?

Answer: ____ ____ ____ ____ ____ ____ ____ ____ ____ ____ ____ ____

" ____ ____ ____ ____ ____ ____ "

Name: _____

Daniel's Ducks

He wanted to grow "mashed" potatoes!

Did you hear about the farmer who plowed his field with a steamroller?

Multiply to find each product.

1. Daniel has 5 pastures on his farm. Each pasture has 4 horses in it. How many horses does Daniel have?

2. Daniel has 3 ponds. There are 5 ducks swimming in each pond. How many ducks does Daniel have?

3. Daniel has 5 goats. He gives each goat 2 apples a day. How many eggs does Daniel gather each day?

4. Daniel counts 4 frogs on each lily pad in a pond. If the pond has 4 lily pads, how many frogs are in the pond?

Rib-Ticklers Math

© Carson-Dellosa • CD-104285

Division Mission

Divide each set of objects into 2 equal groups. Then, solve each division problem.

1.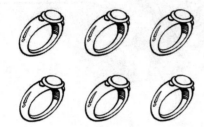

    $6 \div 2 =$ _____

2.

    $4 \div 2 =$ _____

3.

    $8 \div 2 =$ _____

4.

    $2 \div 2 =$ _____

5.

    $14 \div 2 =$ _____

6.

    $10 \div 2 =$ _____

7.

    $16 \div 2 =$ _____

8.

    $20 \div 2 =$ _____

Name: _____

Share and Share Alike

Keyana is sharing a fruit basket with her two best friends. Help her figure out how to split the fruit evenly. Divide each set of objects into 3 equal groups. Then, solve each division problem.

1. $3 \div 3 =$

2. $6 \div 3 =$

3. $9 \div 3 =$

4. $12 \div 3 =$

5. $15 \div 3 =$

6. $18 \div 3 =$

Name: _____

Animal Escape

**Some animals snuck out of the zoo! Help Robert find the missing animals.
Use colorful crayons to connect the problems to their answers. Write the
three letters in order on the answer lines. Then, circle the missing animals
in the picture. The first one has been done for you.**

A. $8 \div 2$	L. ▪▪ ▪▪		K. 2 _____
Y. $6 \div 3$	A. ▲▲▲		L. 3 _____
E. $4 \div 2$	W. ●●●		E. 4 **APE**
O. $9 \div 3$	O. ▲▲▲▲ ▲▲▲▲		X. 6 _____
F. $12 \div 2$	P. ▪▪▪ ▪▪▪		K. 2 _____

Rib-Ticklers Math 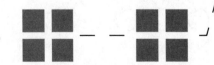 **54**  © Carson-Dellosa • CD-104285

This Little Piggy

Divide to find each quotient.

1. Hannah has 16 pigs. She wants to build enough pens to put 2 pigs in each pen. How many pens does she need to build?

2. Hannah has 9 carrots. She feeds each of her 3 horses an equal number of carrots. How many carrots does each horse get?

3. Hannah has 8 cows. She divides the cows equally into 2 fields. How many cows are in each field?

4. Hannah harvests 12 pumpkins from her pumpkin vines. If each vine has 2 pumpkins, how many pumpkin vines does she have?

Water, Water Everywhere

Addition and multiplication problems are commutative. This means that you can switch the order of the numbers being added or multiplied, and it will not change the answer.

$$4 + 2 = 6 \text{ is the same as } 2 + 4 = 6$$
$$4 \times 2 = 8 \text{ is the same as } 2 \times 4 = 8$$

Match problems that are commutative and cross out the letters beside them. To solve the riddle, write the remaining letters in order on the answer lines.

S	1 + 6	9 x 5	**T**	
O	2 x 2	2 + 1	**U**	
N	7 + 1	5 x 3	**R**	
T	7 x 9	4 + 3	**N**	
A	5 x 8	6 + 4	**R**	
A	1 + 2	9 x 7	**X**	
L	4 + 6	6 + 6	**M**	
W	5 x 9	6 + 1	**O**	
A	2 x 1	1 + 7	**K**	
G	3 x 5	9 + 7	**P**	

Where can you find an ocean with no water?

Answer: ____ ____   ____ ____ ____

Movers and Shakers

Use the key to write addition and subtraction problems. Find each sum or difference. To solve the riddle, match the answers to the numbers below.

$$\square = 5 \qquad \triangle = 6 \qquad \bigcirc = 9 \qquad \boxed{} = 13 \qquad \bigcirc\!\!\!\!\bigcirc = 18$$
$$\heartsuit = 19 \qquad \star = 22 \qquad \diamondsuit = 12 \qquad \pentagon = 15$$

1. ⬡ − ○ = _____ **I**   2. △ − □ = _____ **A**

3. ○ + △ = _____ **O**   4. ☆ − ⬠ = _____ **G**

5. ▭ − ○ = _____ **D**   6. □ + △ = _____ **S**

7. ☆ − ♡ = _____ **C**   8. ◇ + △ = _____ **R**

9. ⬡ − □ = _____ **E**   10. ⬠ + □ = _____ **T**

How do you make a milk shake?

Answer: Give   ___ ___ ___
                  9   20   1

___ ___ ___ ___   ___ ___ ___ ___ ___.
7   15   15   4   11   3   1   18   5

Music to My Ears

Draw the next shape in each pattern. To solve the riddle, match the answers to the shapes below. Then, write the correct letter on each answer line.

1. □ □ □ □ □ _____ **H**

2. 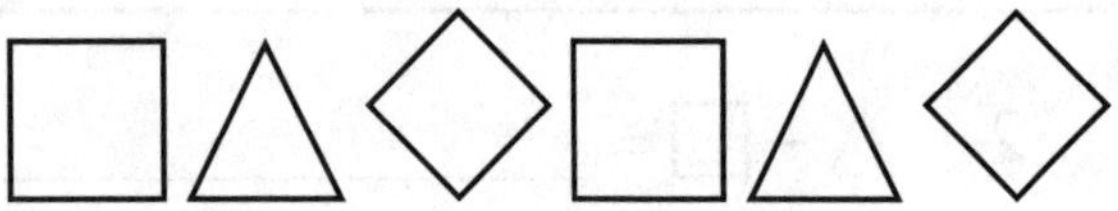 □ △ ◇ ◇ □ △ ◇ _____ **E**

3. 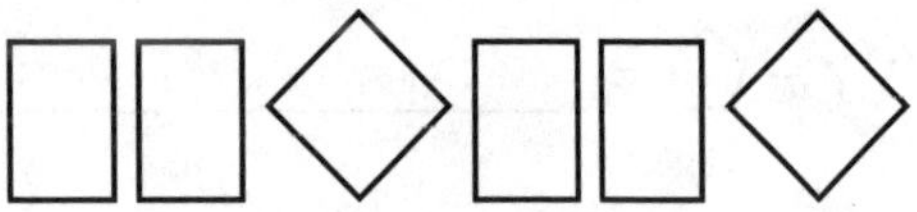 □ □ ◇ □ □ ◇ _____ **Y**

4.  O D □ D O D □ D _____ **T**

5. 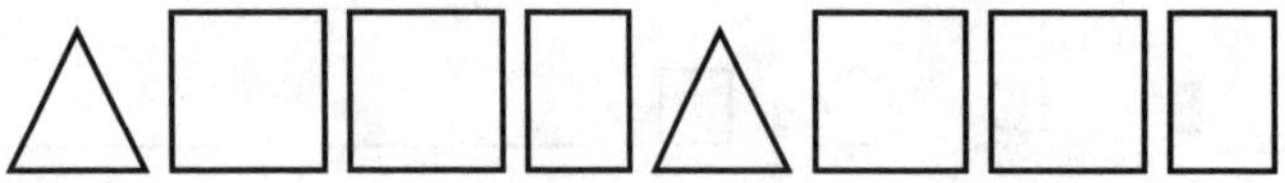 △ □ □ □ △ □ □ _____ **L**

6.  D □ □ △ D □ □ △ _____ **V**

7. 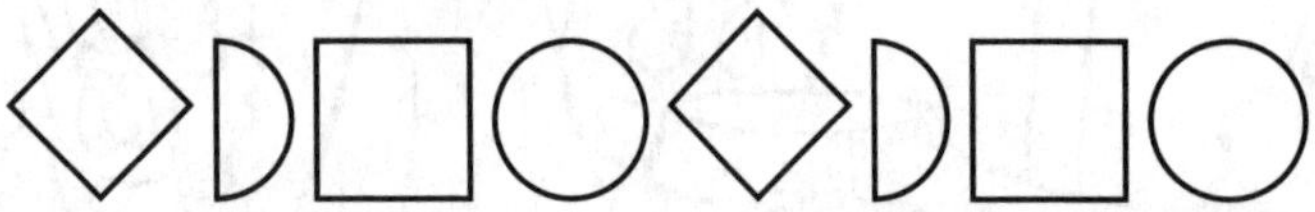 ◇ D □ O ◇ ◇ D □ O _____ **A**

8. 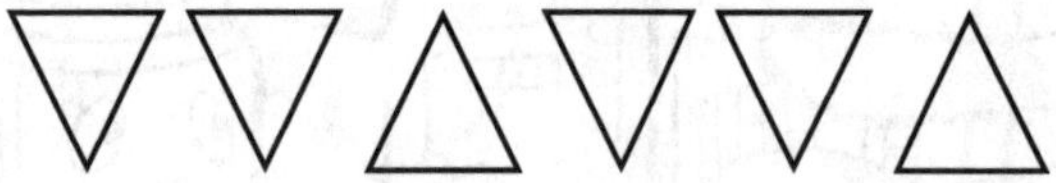 ▽ ▽ ▽ △ ▽ ▽ △ _____ **M**

What kind of music weighs the most?

Answer: " ___ ___ ___ ___ ___   ___ ___ ___ ___ ___ "
□ □ ◇ D □   ▽ □ O ◇ △

Top Dog

Find the pattern of each set of letters or numbers. Match sets with the same pattern. To solve the riddle, write the letters in order on the answer lines.

1. A, B, C, A, B, C   E. 3, 2, 1, 3, 2, 1

2. A, B, B, A, B, B   F. 1, 2, 3, 1, 2, 3

3. B, A, A, B, A, A   R. 1, 1, 2, 1, 1, 2

4. A, B, A, B, A, B   L. 1, 2, 2, 1, 2, 2

5. C, B, A, C, B, A   O. 2, 1, 1, 2, 1, 1

6. A, A, B, A, A, B   W. 1, 2, 1, 2, 1, 2

What do you get when you cross a dog with a daisy?

Answer: A

" C O L L I E . ___ ___ ___ ___ ___ ___ ___ ___ "

Munching on Math

Draw the next shape in each pattern.

1.

2.

3.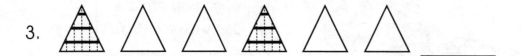

4.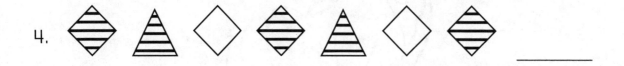

5.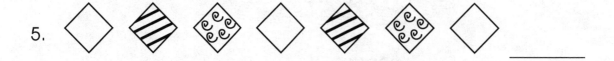

Gwen's Garden

Someone has been eating the carrots in Gwen's garden! Help her find out who it is. Write the missing number in each equation. Match each missing number with the correct color in the key. Then, color each space below. The picture will solve the mystery.

6 = blue	13 = gray	10 = green
14 = orange	15 = pink	

$10 + \underline{\quad} = 16$

$\underline{\quad} + 7 = 13$

$2 + \underline{\quad} = 15$

$\underline{\quad} + 3 = 16$

$2 + \underline{\quad} = 17$

$\underline{\quad} + 3 = 18$

$5 + \underline{\quad} = 18$

$8 + \underline{\quad} = 14$

$\underline{\quad} + 13 = 19$

$6 + \underline{\quad} = 19$

$\underline{\quad} + 4 = 19$

$\underline{\quad} + 7 = 20$

$5 + \underline{\quad} = 20$

$4 + \underline{\quad} = 14$

$\underline{\quad} + 4 = 17$

$\underline{\quad} + 6 = 16$

$\underline{\quad} + 2 = 16$

$\underline{\quad} + 5 = 19$

$\underline{\quad} + 1 = 14$

$8 + \underline{\quad} = 21$

A Head above the Rest

Write the missing number in each equation. Match each missing number with the correct color in the key. Then, color each space below. The picture will solve the riddle.

8 = brown	9 = yellow	10 = red
11 = green	12 = blue	

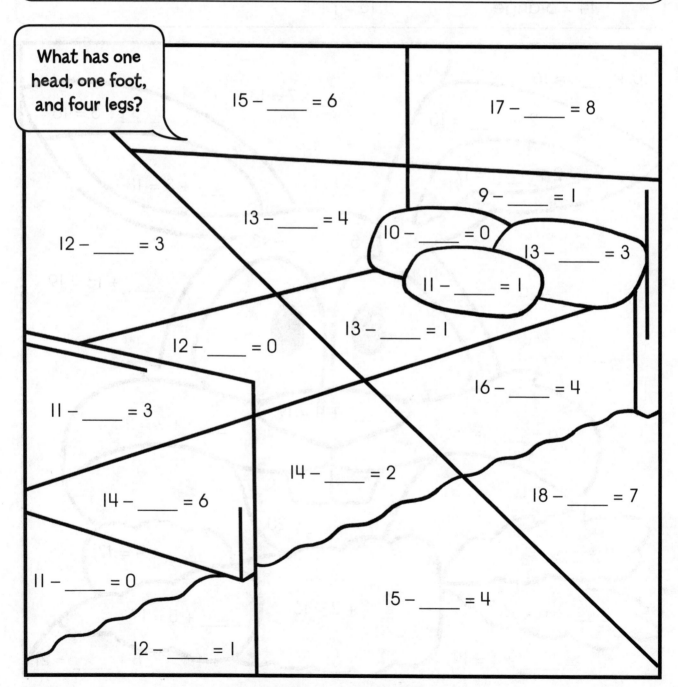

What has one head, one foot, and four legs?

$15 - \underline{} = 6$

$17 - \underline{} = 8$

$13 - \underline{} = 4$

$9 - \underline{} = 1$

$10 - \underline{} = 0$

$13 - \underline{} = 3$

$12 - \underline{} = 3$

$11 - \underline{} = 1$

$12 - \underline{} = 0$

$13 - \underline{} = 1$

$16 - \underline{} = 4$

$11 - \underline{} = 3$

$14 - \underline{} = 2$

$14 - \underline{} = 6$

$18 - \underline{} = 7$

$11 - \underline{} = 0$

$15 - \underline{} = 4$

$12 - \underline{} = 1$

Excuse the Elephant

Write the missing number in each equation. To solve the riddle, match each answer with the correct letter in the key. Then, write the letters in order on the answer lines.

2 = V	7 = S	8 = I	9 = O	10 = M
3 = E	4 = H	5 = F	6 = T	

1. $14 - \underline{\hspace{1cm}} = 4$ 2. $11 + \underline{\hspace{1cm}} = 19$ 3. $7 + \underline{\hspace{1cm}} = 14$

4. $10 - \underline{\hspace{1cm}} = 3$ 5. $5 + \underline{\hspace{1cm}} = 15$ 6. $16 - \underline{\hspace{1cm}} = 7$

7. $12 + \underline{\hspace{1cm}} = 19$ 8. $18 - \underline{\hspace{1cm}} = 12$ 9. $8 + \underline{\hspace{1cm}} = 17$

10. $13 + \underline{\hspace{1cm}} = 18$ 11. $9 + \underline{\hspace{1cm}} = 15$ 12. $12 - \underline{\hspace{1cm}} = 8$

13. $16 + \underline{\hspace{1cm}} = 19$ 14. $6 + \underline{\hspace{1cm}} = 16$ 15. $17 - \underline{\hspace{1cm}} = 8$

16. $9 - \underline{\hspace{1cm}} = 7$ 17. $15 - \underline{\hspace{1cm}} = 7$ 18. $11 + \underline{\hspace{1cm}} = 14$

What would you do if an elephant sat in front of you at a theater?

Answer: ___ ___ ___ ___   ___ ___ ___

___ ___   ___ ___ ___   ___ ___ ___

Polly Wants a Cracker

Write the missing information.

Name	Picture	Number of Sides	Definition
Triangle			
			a polygon with 4 equal sides and 4 right angles
	▭		
		5	
Hexagon			
	⬡		

Name: _____

Great Shapes

Identify each shape and write its name on the line. Then, find each name in the word search.

1.
_____

2.
_____

3.
_____

4.
_____

5.
_____

6.
_____

7.
_____

8.
_____

9.
_____

10.
_____

11.
_____

12.
_____

```
r  h  e  p  t  a  g  o  n  r  w  z  h  p  s
h  h  i  q  u  g  p  z  n  y  o  m  t  e  q
o  e  v  d  e  c  a  g  o  n  r  p  r  n  u
m  x  w  e  q  i  y  h  n  e  f  p  i  t  a
b  a  p  t  n  r  d  j  a  t  k  s  a  a  r
u  g  i  x  e  c  v  s  g  b  j  r  n  g  e
s  o  a  l  m  l  f  m  o  c  t  a  g  o  n
g  n  d  z  q  e  p  i  n  u  e  g  l  n  d
r  e  c  t  a  n  g  l  e  a  c  n  e  u  q
y  f  t  s  w  t  r  a  p  e  z  o  i  d  c
```

All four-sided polygons are called _____.

Name a four-sided polygon with parallel opposite sides. _____

Out of This World

Color all of the triangles blue. Color all of the rectangles green. Color all of the circles yellow.

Name: _____   congruent shapes

That Is a Wrap!

Match the congruent shapes. To solve the riddle, write the letters in order on the lines below. The first one has been done for you.

1.   A.

2. 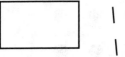   C.

3.   I.

4.   M.

5.   P.

6.   R.

7.   S.

8.   U.

9.   W.

What music do mummies like?

Answer: "_W_ ___ ___ ___" ___ ___ ___

Rib-Ticklers Math   **67**   © Carson-Dellosa • CD-104285

Symona's Symmetrical Shapes

Symona has drawn half of each shape. Draw the other half of each shape so that the shape is symmetrical.

1.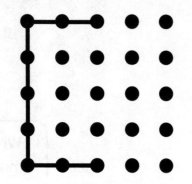

2.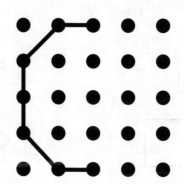

3.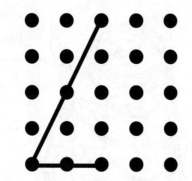

4.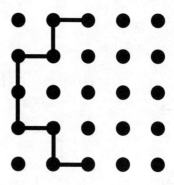

5.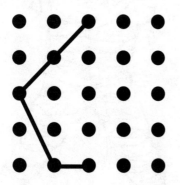

6.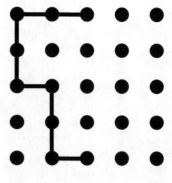

7.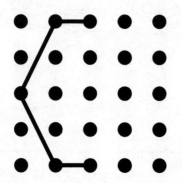

8.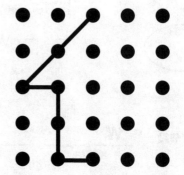

Name: _____

Mark's Marvelous Map

Write the coordinates for each location.

Mark drew a map of his neighborhood on a grid. He placed his house at 0. Now, he needs to write where everything is. To make things clear, he needs to write how many blocks east (or across) first, then how many blocks north (or up). For example, the statue is located at (1, 2). To get there from his house, Mark walks 1 block east and 2 blocks north.

1. school: _____   2. park: _____

3. toy store: _____   4. Mark's house: _____

5. movie theater: _____   6. pool: _____

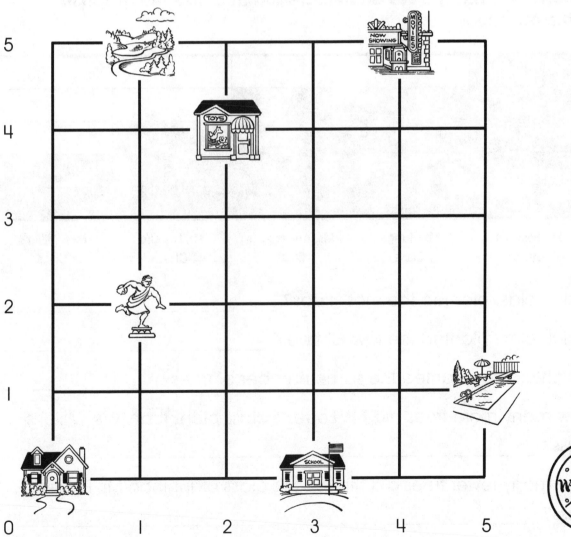

Name: _____

"Tree-mendous" Work

Sunny Grove Elementary School planted trees for Earth Day. The graph below shows how many trees each class planted. Use the graph to answer the questions.

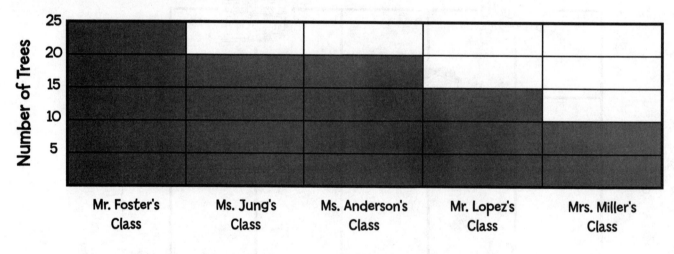

1. Which class planted the most trees? _____

2. Which class planted the fewest trees? _____

3. Which classes planted the same number of trees? _____

4. How many more trees did Mr. Lopez's class plant than Mrs. Miller's class? _____

5. How many fewer trees did Mr. Lopez's class plant than Mr. Foster's class? _____

Rib-Ticklers Math **70** © Carson-Dellosa • CD-104285

All Aboard!

Why do railroad workers have great hearing?

Because they have "engine-ears!"

Lisa polled her classmates to find out what they would like to be when they grow up. She graphed her results below. Use the graph to answer the questions.

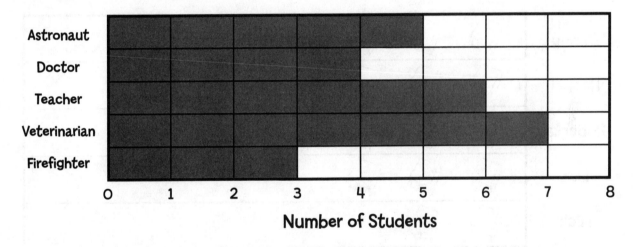

Number of Students

1. How many students did Lisa poll? _____

2. How many students chose *veterinarian*? _____

3. Did more students choose *astronaut* or *teacher*? _____

4. How many more students said that they wanted to be a veterinarian than a firefighter? _____

5. How many students said that they wanted to be a doctor, a teacher, or an astronaut? _____

Reading between the Lines

Five friends made a pictograph to show how many books they read in 1 month. Use the graph to answer the questions.

Number of Books Read

Danny	📖	📖	📖	📖	
Rachel	📖	📖	📖		
Roberta	📖	📖	📖	📖	📖
Lisa	📖	📖	📖		
Nick	📖	📖			

📖 = 1 book

1. Who read the most books? _____

2. Who read the fewest books? _____

3. Who read the same amount of books as Rachel? _____

4. How many more books did Roberta read than Lisa? _____

5. How many total books were read? _____

Name: _____

Grab Bag Goodies

Hailey and Morgan both received an A+ on the last math test of the year. As a reward, they each get to pick one prize out of three grab bags. What are Hailey's and Morgan's chances of getting each item? Look at each picture. Label each option as *least likely*, *most likely*, *same chance*, or *no chance*.

1. apple: _____

2. orange: _____

3. pear: _____

4. ball: _____

5. yo-yo: _____

6. marbles: _____

7. smiley face sticker: _____

8. star sticker: _____

9. heart sticker: _____

Rib-Ticklers Math

© Carson-Dellosa • CD-104285

Page 4

1. thirteen; 2. forty-two; 3. eighty-seven;
4. one hundred six; 5. two hundred;
6. three hundred ten; 7. four hundred;
8. five hundred; 9. eight hundred;
10. one thousand

Page 5

1. 33, 92, 103, 220, 99, 127, 153, 172, shoe glue;
2. 201, 234, 250, 285, 296, 311, 339, 346, pale pail; 3. 364, 367, 376, 377, 414, 425, 440, 499, lawn fawn

Page 6

Page 7

1. seventy-sixth; 2. forty-fifth; 3. thirty-seventh;
4. fifty-ninth; 5. ninety-eighth; 6. sixty-fourth;
7. eightieth; 8. thirteenth; 9. thirtieth;
10. fifty-second

Page 8

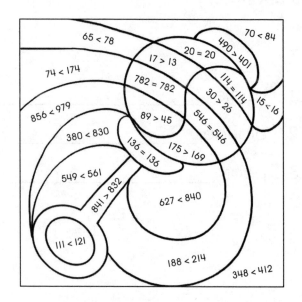

Page 9

1.R; 2. O; 3. C; 4. K; 5. G; 6. R; 7. O; 8. U; 9. P; a "rock" group

Page 10

1. 9; 2. 11; 3. 13; 4. 4; 5. 6; 6. 8; 7. 38; 8. 40;
9. 42; 10. 13; 11. 15; 12. 17; 13. 19; 14. 21; 15. 23;
Because 7 "8" 9.

Page 11

1. 14; 2. 18; 3. 13; 4. 16; 5. 10; 6. 17; 7. 15; 8. 9;
9. 20; 10. 8; 11. 6; 12. 2; 13. 11; 14. 19; 15. 4; with tomato paste

Page 12

1. 55; 2. 79; 3. 55; 4. 90; 5. 86; 6. 90; 7. 55; 8. 82;
9. 56; 10. 79; 11. 81; 12. 68; 13. 82; 14. 94; 15. 27;
He has a "honey-comb."

Page 13

1. 533; 2. 235; 3. 192; 4. 482; 5. 578; 6. 291;
7. 758; 8. 978; 9. 497; 10. 743; 11. 894; 12. 325;
13. 617; 14. 869; He wanted to "play it by ear."

Page 14

1. 179 blocks; 2. 178 birds and monkeys;
3. 309 paintings and sculptures; 4. 80 students

Page 15

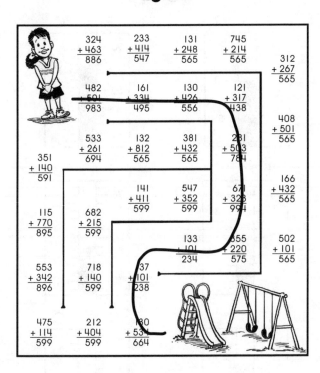

Page 16

1. 21; 2. 42; 3. 40; 4. 20; 5. 33; 6. 31; 7. 30; 8.
32; 9. 88; 10. 45; 11. 43; 12. 41; Because he
thought it was "lion"

Page 17

1. 62; 2. 86; 3. 80; 4. 65; 5. 40; 6. 55; 7. 44; 8. 42;
9. 73; 10. 91; 11. 60; time to get a new car

Page 18

1. 42 apples; 2. 70 pears; 3. 31 pies; 4. 81 trees

Page 19

1. 100; 2. 185; 3. 291; 4. 249; 5. 601; 6. 526;
7. 318; 8. 388; 9. 225; 10. 698; 11. 618; 12. 339;
13. 828; 14. 730; 15. 964; Because he wanted
a "cool" ride

Page 20

Across: 2. 951; 3. 812; 4. 465; 7. 913; 9. 771;
11. 649; 12. 281; 13. 308; Down: 1. 291; 2. 924;
3. 861; 5. 573; 6. 416; 8. 338; 10. 590; 12. 280;
13. 340

Page 21

1. 81 cherries and grapes; 2. 131 granola
bars and apples; 3. 270 carrot sticks;
4. 268 jelly beans

Page 22

1. 18; 2. 10; 3. 6; 4. 9; 5. 16; 6. 11; 7. 15; 8. 14;
9. 7; 10. 12; 11. 8; 12. 13; in "pocket"
dictionaries

Page 23

1. 43 bean stalks; 2. 10 sunflower seeds;
3. 12 tomato plants; 4. 11 strawberries

Page 24

1. 44; 2. 12; 3. 56; 4. 14; 5. 25; 6. 29; 7. 23;
8. 33; 9. 44; 10. 31; 11. 61; 12. 72; 13. 50; a flying
"car-pet"

Page 25

1. 610; 2. 330; 3. 121; 4. 330; 5. 542; 6. 51;
7. 404; 8. 105; 9. 542; 10. 334; 11. 142; 12. 51;
13. 313; 14. 514; 15. 529; the "hound" of music

Page 26

1. 14 miles; 2. 730 people; 3. 651 people;
4. 161 people

Page 27

1. 12; 2. 18; 3. 18; 4. 13; 5. 16; 6. 19; 7. 29; 8. 28; 9. 19; 10. 19; 11. 26; 12. 29; cookie "sheets"

Page 28

1. 11; 2. 29; 3. 24; 4. 14; 5. 19; 6. 19; 7. 18; 8. 9; 9. 24; 10. 9; 11. 8; 12. 13; in a "moos-paper"

Page 29

1. 9 hummingbirds; 2. 12 red roses; 3. 6 flowers; 4. 9 ladybugs

Page 30

1. 83; 2. 313; 3. 709; 4. 532; 5. 246; 6. 818; 7. 114; 8. 226; 9. 439; 10. 105; 11. 148; 12. 91; a cow on a bicycle

Page 31

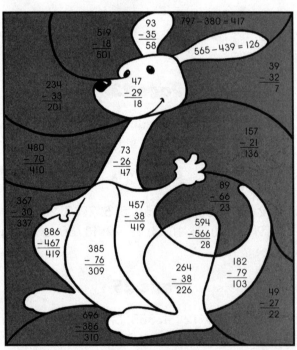

Page 32

1. 19 cookies; 2. 205 cookies; 3. 291 muffins; 4. 498 sugar cookies

Page 33

1. 10 yd.; 2. 16 ft.; 3. 18 ft.; 4. 40 yd.; 5. 24 ft.; 6. 20 ft.; 7. 16 yd.; 8. 28 ft.

Page 34

1. 90°F, 32°C shorts, flip-flops, T-shirt; 2. 50°F, 10°C, jacket, tennis shoes; 3. 30°F, -1°C, winter coat, scarf, hat; 4. 70°F, 21°C, jeans, T-shirt

Page 35

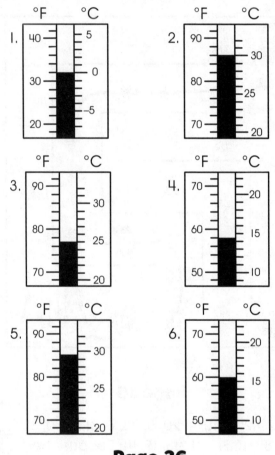

Page 36

1. in.; 2. ft.; 3. yd.; 4. ft.; 5. in.; 6. ft.; 7. ft.; 8. yd.; 9. in.

Page 37

1. cm; 2. m; 3. m; 4. cm; 5. cm; 6. cm; 7. m; 8. cm; 9. m

Page 38

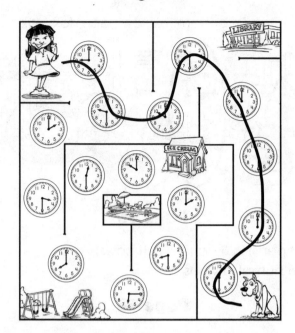

Page 39

Page 40

1. 9:50; 2. 2:25; 3. 9:10; 4. 6:55; 5. 2:45; 6. 10:20;
7. 5:40; ten after one

Page 41

1. 4:10; 2. 10:55; 3. 1:35; 4. 3:05; 5. 3:25; 6. 6:50;
7. 11:20; 8. 2:15; 9. 4:45; a "suit" of armor

Page 42

1. 2:00; 2. 2:15; 3. 1:15; 4. 0:30; 5. 2:30; 6. 1:45;
7. 2:20; It needed a "hand."

Page 43

1. Monday; 2. 4; 3. Saturday, February 26;
4. Tuesday; 5. February 8

Page 44

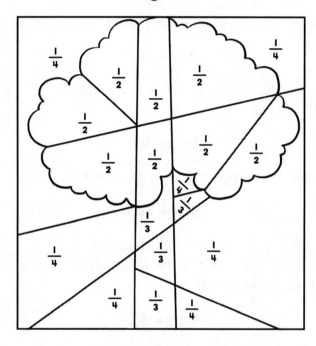

Page 45

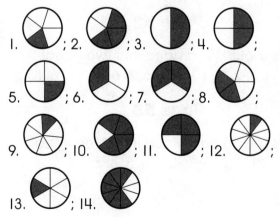

Page 46

1. $\frac{1}{2}$; 2. $\frac{3}{4}$; 3. $\frac{1}{5}$; 4. $\frac{1}{3}$; 5. $\frac{1}{4}$; 6. $\frac{3}{5}$;

7. $\frac{2}{3}$; 8. $\frac{1}{6}$; 9. $\frac{4}{5}$; 10. $\frac{1}{5}$; 11. $\frac{5}{6}$; It took the

wrong "root."

Page 47

1. <; 2. =; 3. <; 4. <; 5. =; 6. >; 7. >; 8. <; 9. >; 10. <; 11. >; 12. <; your front teeth

Page 48

1. 4; 2. 10; 3. 9; 4. 6; 5. 8; 6. 8; 7. 12; 8. 12; Pictures will vary.

Page 49

From top to bottom: jam; gum; pie; tea; egg

Page 50

1. 15; 2. 8; 3. 25; 4. 27; 5. 10; 6. 50; 7. 16; 8. 12; 9. 21; 10. 20; 11. 32; 12. 40; 13. 35; 14. 45; 15. 28; 16. 18; when it is a "sea lion"

Page 51

1. 20 horses; 2. 15 ducks; 3. 10 apples; 4. 16 frogs

Page 52

Objects should be divided into two equal groups. 1. 3; 2. 2; 3. 4; 4. 1; 5. 7; 6. 5; 7. 8; 8. 10

Page 53

Objects should be divided into three equal groups. 1. 1; 2. 2; 3. 3; 4. 4; 5. 5; 6. 6

Page 54

From top to bottom: elk; owl; ape; fox; yak;

Page 55

1. 8 pens; 2. 3 carrots; 3. 4 cows; 4. 6 pumpkin vines

Page 56

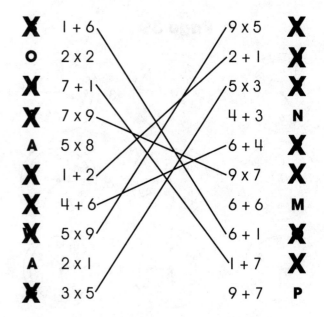

on a map

Page 57

1. $18 - 9 = 9$; 2. $6 - 5 = 1$; 3. $9 + 6 = 15$; 4. $22 - 15 = 7$; 5. $13 - 9 = 4$; 6. $5 + 6 = 11$; 7. $22 - 19 = 3$; 8. $12 + 6 = 18$; 9. $18 - 13 = 5$; 10. $15 + 5 = 20$; Give it a good scare.